The History Nook

by Lisa Lerner

Illustrated by Tom Newsom

It's a beautiful day in the year 2050. The Woodley twins aren't playing football or cooking up snacks as they often do after class. Today, Brooke and Booker are doing research for their class project. They have to prepare a report about communication in the time before there were computers. Mom will pick them up from the Woodside Library in a few hours.

"We've got a lot to learn," says Booker. "We'd better get going."

"Where do we begin?" Brooke asks. "The past is a lot of time to cover!"

WOODSIDE PUBLIC LIBRARY

"I have an idea," Booker says. "Let's ask the research computer. Maybe we will find a few ideas to help us get started."

"Good thinking," says Brooke, getting the computer going with a few commands. Then she asks it, "How can I learn about communication in the time before computers?"

The computer is not a person, but it replies with a simple sentence: *"Take a look in the History Nook."*

WELCOME...
I'M YOUR LIBRARY
RESEARCH
CHOOSE VOCAL OR KEYBOARD FORMAT
V K
READY
TO BEGIN
TOUCH ANY KEY

The twins look around. "Where is the History Nook?" Booker asks. Ms. Goodman, who works in the research area, comes over to help. The twins tell her about their project. Ms. Goodman checks the computer and prints out some places and dates. "Ask the History Nook to let you view these," she says, "and you'll find out a lot about communication." Then she takes the twins over to the History Nook.

the
HISTORY
Time: 1440

Inside, they see seats that look a bit like desks, each with a few buttons and a control stick.

"You may speak your commands the way you do with most computers," Ms. Goodman tells them. "Or, you may write your commands." She shows the twins the way to use the controls.

When the twins are seated, Ms. Goodman says, "Remember, with the History Nook program we will view scenes from the past. When the room lights go off, Booker can write the first command."

The controls glow in the dark as Booker writes a few words from Ms. Goodman's list on his command screen:

Time: 1440
Place: Germany

Suddenly, they see a chilly place filled with wooden tables and odd-looking machines.

"What's going on?" asks Brooke. She uses her controls to get a closer view.

"Look," says Booker, "that man is moving some small metal letters. Maybe he's trying to write a word or a sentence with them."

"Why don't you ask the History Nook program to tell us what we're viewing?" Ms. Goodman says.

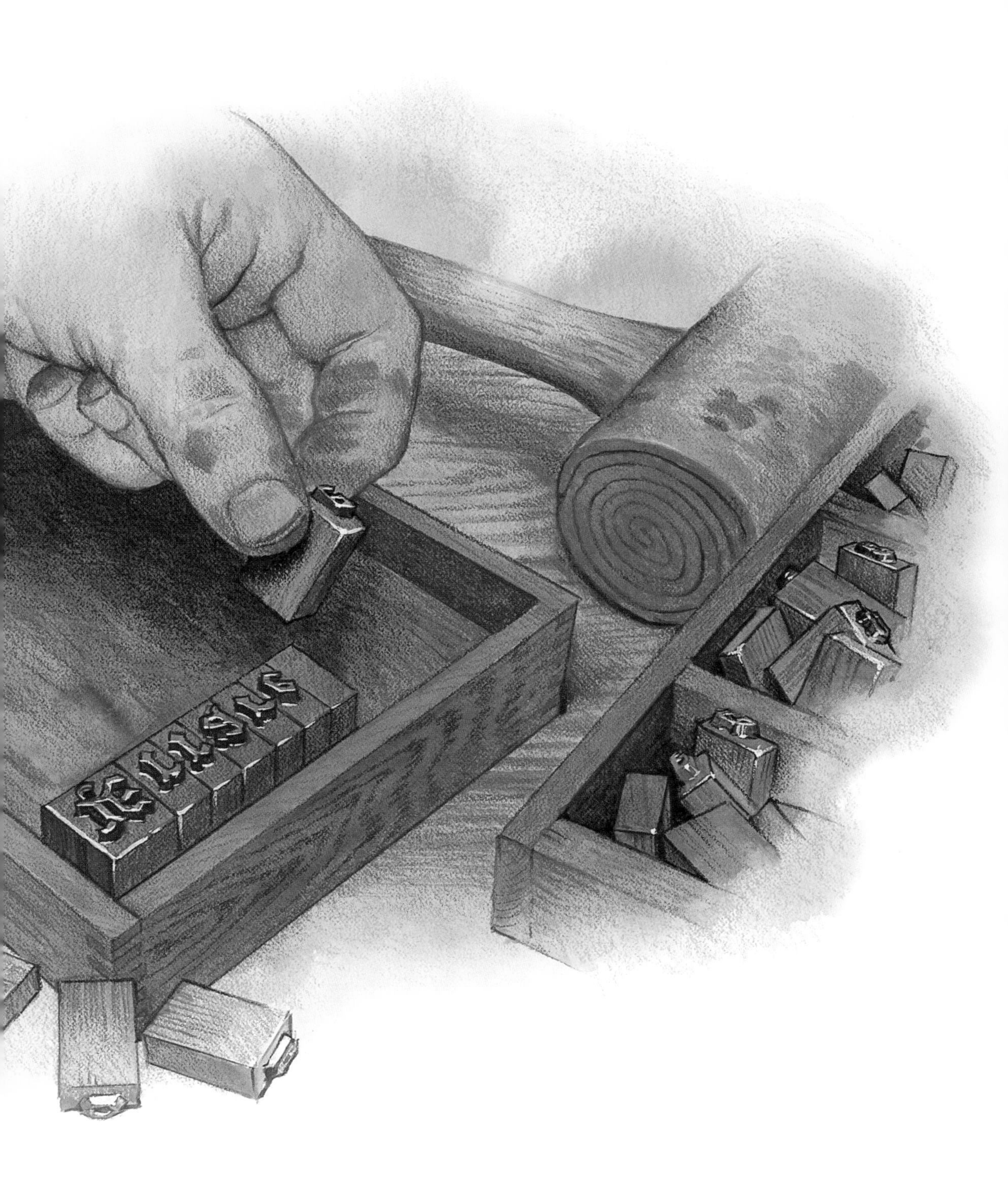

Brooke gives the command,
and the History Nook speaker begins:

"Johann Gutenberg has come up with a new way of making books. People don't have to write every sentence by hand anymore like they used to. This is the biggest change since writing began.

Gutenberg has made metal letters that line up to make words and sentences. Then, he puts ink on the letters and presses a paper over them with his new machine, the printing press. It is a lot easier and faster to make books in this way. Now more people can have books."

"It looks like people have been making books for a long time," Booker says. "I wonder when people learned other ways to communicate."

"Let's try the next date," says Ms. Goodman.

Brooke copies these words onto her command screen:

Time: 1876
Place: Boston, Massachusetts

The next view they see is of a place that looks like an old-time lab. A man is sitting at a desk. There is a battery and an odd-shaped machine on the desk. The man bumps the battery. It tips off the desk. Something wet spills from the battery onto the man's pants. He jumps up and yells, "Mr. Watson, come here. I want you!"

Suddenly, another man runs in. "I heard you, Mr. Bell!" the second man yells. "Your voice went over the wire! Your machine is working at last!"

“Watson, we’ve done it!” Mr. Bell says as they shake hands.

The twins look at each other, confused, as they both say, “Let’s ask what they’ve done!”

Booker gives the command,
and the History Nook speaker explains:

"After many years of trying, Alexander Graham Bell and his assistant, Thomas Watson, have just made the first telephone. It uses wires to carry people's words. Finally, people who are far away from each other have a way to talk together. The telephone makes another big change in communication."

"That's a telephone?" Brooke asks. "Where's the viewer? Can't you see the person you're speaking to?"

"That's the way old telephones were," Ms. Goodman says. "Telephones haven't always had viewers, you know."

"I didn't know that," Booker says. "I guess that's another thing we've learned about communication before the computer."

"Let's see what comes after the telephone," Brooke says as she writes the next command:

Time: 1939
Place: New York City

"Look at all the people! I wonder what's going on," says Booker.

"They are all looking at that black-and-white screen over there," says Brooke. "Let's get closer to hear what people are saying."

"This is the best thing at the World's Fair!" a man says. "What is it called?"

"It's called a television," someone says.

"Let's ask History Nook to tell us more," says Booker, as he gives a command.

The speaker begins:

"A new machine called a television is shown to the people of the world at the 1939 World's Fair. People are finally able to see the news. Before, they could only hear it on the radio."

“What’s a radio?” Booker asks.

“We don’t have time to learn today,” Brooke says, looking at her watch. “Mom is probably waiting for us!”

“Ask your mom,” Ms. Goodman says. “I’m sure she remembers what a radio is.”

“We really did learn a lot,” says Brooke. “It’s been fun doing research for our project. Thanks for showing us the History Nook.”

“Come back any time,” Ms. Goodman says.

“We will!” Booker exclaims. “I think we’re hooked on history!”

The History of Communications

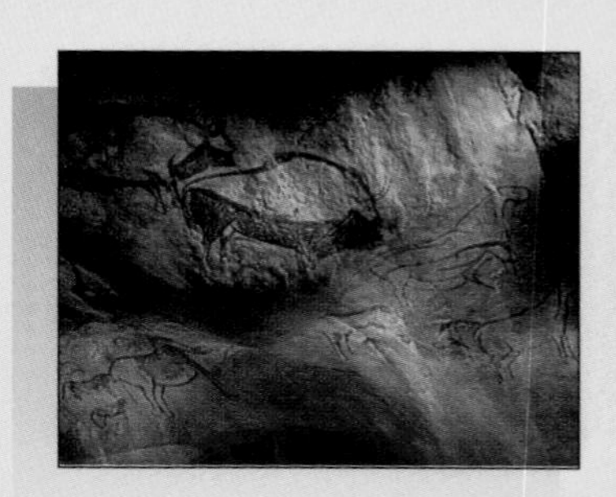

Cave Drawings
20,000 – 10,000 B.C.

Handwritten Books
400 – 1,000 A.D.

Telegraph
1830

1,500 B.C.
Pictographic Writing

1440
Printing Press

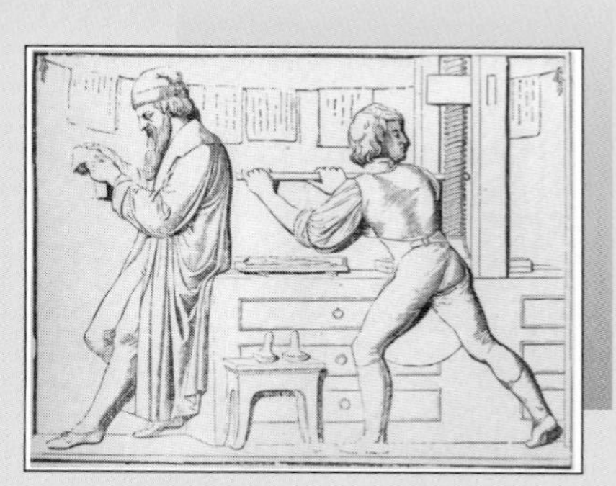

1876
Telephone